THE IRISH HERITAGE COOKBOOK

By Mercedes McLoughlin and Marian McSpiritt

TRiBECA
COMMUNICATIONS, INC.

New York

This edition of THE IRISH HERITAGE COOKBOOK is published under license from Careers and Educational Publishers Ltd., Lower James Street, Claremorris, Co. Mayo, Ireland, who first published this work in Ireland in 1983.

Library of Congress Cataloging in Publication Data

McLoughlin, Mercedes.
   The Irish heritage cookbook.

   1. Cookery, Irish. I. McSpiritt, Marian. II. Title.
TX717.5.M34 1984   641.59415   83-24346

ISBN 0-943392-41-1

Distributed in Canada by Prentice-Hall Canada Inc., 1870 Birchmount Road, Scarborough, Ontario M1P 2J7

Printed in the United States of America
First Edition: February 1984

1 2 3 4 5 6 7 8 9 10

ACKNOWLEDGMENTS

We owe a special debt to these members of our family who contributed recipes and inspiration:

Mary Bourke
Mary Hanley Bourke
Emily Gillespie
Irene Gillespie
Grace Glynn
Catherine Kelleher
James Kelleher
Meighan Kelleher
Mary MacNeely
Bridget Madden
Kathleen Mangan
Katie Mangan
Anita McCudden
Patrick McCudden
Theresa McGowan
Annie McLoughlin
Fionna O'Bierne
Angela Padden
Theresa Reape
Jacqueline Rudman
Laura Rudman

AN IRISH RECIPE!

INGREDIENTS:

> Four cups of love
> Two cups of loyalty
> Three cups of friendship

Take love and loyalty and mix it thoroughly with faith; blend it with tenderness, kindness and understanding; add hope, sprinkle abundantly with laughter and bake it with sunshine.

Serve generous helpings daily to your family, friends and all you meet.

INTRODUCTION

We have collected these recipes from our family in Ireland who have welcomed us into their homes many times with typical hospitality and fine cooking.

It is a collection of some of the foods served in homes in Ireland and is a combination of traditional and present day recipes.

We hope these recipes will add to your enjoyment and enhance your appreciation of food as part of the heritage and culture of Ireland.

Mercedes McLoughlin
Marian McSpiritt

TABLE OF CONTENTS

AFTERS 79

STARTERS

Eggs Mayonnaise

INGREDIENTS:

> 1 egg per serving
> ½ cup of heavy cream
> Salt and pepper
> Lemon juice or vinegar
> ¼ cup mayonnaise
> 2 tablespoons chopped parsley
> Garden Lettuce

Place eggs in a saucepan, cover completely with cold water. Place over low heat and bring slowly to the boiling point. Reduce heat and simmer for 12 to 15 minutes. Stir occasionally to keep yolks in the center of the egg. Remove from heat and submerge in cold water immediately. When eggs are cooled remove shell. Cut egg in half lengthwise and carefully remove the yolk.

Crush the yolks and add 1 tablespoon heavy cream for each yolk. Season to taste with salt and pepper, vinegar or lemon juice. Fill centers of eggs with yolk mixture. Garnish top with 1 teaspoon of mayonnaise and a sprinkling of chopped parsley. Serve on a bed of garden lettuce.

Galway Bay Oysters

INGREDIENTS:

> 6 oysters per serving
> Crushed ice
> Lemon wedges
> Whole-grain bread (p.73)
> Butter

Arrange opened oysters on a bed of crushed ice. Garnish with lemon wedges.

Serve with whole-grain bread and butter.

Dublin Bay Prawn Cocktail

INGREDIENTS:

Prawns—6 large prawns or shrimp per person
Shredded lettuce
Cocktail sauce:
    ½ cup heavy cream, whipped
    1 teaspoon tarragon
    ¼ teaspoon Dijon mustard
    1 teaspoon chopped chives
    Salt and pepper to taste

Cook, peel and devein the prawns. Shred the lettuce. Arrange the prawns on the shredded lettuce. Pour 1 to 2 tablespoons of sauce over each serving.

Sauce: Whip cream, add tarragon, mustard and chives, salt and pepper. Blend well and chill.

Seafood Cocktail Mulraney

INGREDIENTS:

1 lb. fish fillets: whiting, haddock and/or cod
1 cup mayonnaise
1½ tablespoons tomato catsup
Dash of Worcestershire sauce
4 tablespoons beaten cream
1 tablespoon lemon juice
Salt and pepper to taste
Lettuce
Lemon wedges

Place fish in boiling salted water. Bring to boil again and simmer steadily for 3-5 minutes. Drain thoroughly and allow to cool. Chill.

Mix tomato catsup with mayonnaise, add other ingredients and stir until well blended.

Cut fish into bite-sized pieces and arrange on a bed of crisp greens. Spoon the dressing over the fish and garnish with lemon wedges.

Killala Bay Shellfish Cocktail

INGREDIENTS:

½ lb. cooked shelled shrimp
¾ lb. poached monkfish, cut into bite sized pieces
½ lb. cooked crabmeat, picked over
Cocktail sauce:
⅓ cup oil
¼ cup vinegar
1 clove garlic, crushed
2 tablespoons each chopped parsley and chives
1 tablespoon chopped tarragon
Salt and pepper
Lettuce
Tomato wedges
Lemon slice

Combine cooked fish in a large bowl. Mix all ingredients for sauce together. Pour over fish, toss and marinate for two hours in refrigerator.

Serve on lettuce leaf and garnish with tomato wedges and a slice of lemon.

Cottage Pâté With Red Currant Sauce

INGREDIENTS:

1 lb. chicken livers
4 tablespoons butter or margarine
4 slices of bacon, chopped
1 garlic clove, crushed
1 onion, chopped
¼ teaspoon mace
¼ teaspoon ground cloves
1 egg
1 tablespoon chopped parsley
Salt and pepper to taste
1 bay leaf
Lettuce

For Sauce:
½ cup red currant jelly
2 tablespoons horseradish
Rind and juice of 1 orange
½ teaspoon dry mustard

14

Sauté chicken livers in butter until they lose their pink color. Add bacon, crushed garlic and onion and continue sautéing until lightly browned. Reduce heat and simmer for a few minutes.

Remove from heat and cool, add mace, clove, egg, parsley, salt and pepper. Place mixture in blender or food processor. Blend until smooth.

Butter a 7-inch loaf tin. Fill with mixture and smooth top. Place bay leaf on top. Cover pan with foil and set in a pan of hot water. Bake in preheated oven at 350° for 1½ hours.

Cool to room temperature. Place in refrigerator and chill for 8 hours.

TO MAKE SAUCE: Blend red currant jelly, horseradish, orange juice and rind with dry mustard. Chill.

Unmold pâté and slice. Serve on bed of lettuce accompanied by red currant sauce.

Killary Harbor Mussels With Garlic Butter

INGREDIENTS:

1½ lbs. mussel meat or 3 lbs. mussels
6 tablespoons butter
2 garlic cloves, crushed
Salt and pepper to taste
Juice of one lemon
Lemon wedges
Chopped parsley

TO COOK MUSSELS: Wash thoroughly, scraping the shells with a knife or stiff brush. Change the water several times to remove all sand. Drain.

Place mussels in a heavy saucepan and add 1 cup of water. Cover the pot and allow to steam for 7 minutes until the shells are open wide.

Place mussels in ovenproof dish. If in shell, remove the top shell.

Melt butter, add crushed garlic, lemon juice, freshly ground pepper and blend.

Pour over mussels and place under broiler until golden brown.

Garnish with chopped parsley and lemon wedges.

Irish Creme

INGREDIENTS:

1 14 oz. can of condensed milk
3 eggs
2 teaspoons honey
3 tablespoons chocolate syrup
1¼ cups Irish whiskey
½ pint heavy cream
For the chocolate syrup:
   ½ cup cocoa
   2 teaspoons instant coffee
   ¼ cup light corn syrup
   ¾ cup water
   ⅛ teaspoon salt
   ½ teaspoon vinegar

Combine condensed milk, eggs, honey, chocolate syrup and whiskey in blender. Blend for one minute. Add cream and blend for 1½ minutes.

Refrigerate for at least 24 hours before serving.

To make chocolate syrup:

Combine cocoa, instant coffee, corn syrup, water, salt and vinegar. Blend thoroughly. Heat over direct flame until mixture boils. Simmer for 5 minutes, stirring occasionally. Cool, pour into glass jar and refrigerate. (Makes 1¼ cups)

Irish creme will keep for several weeks if refrigerated.

SOUPS

Dymphna's Celery Soup

INGREDIENTS:

2 cups chopped celery
2 medium onions, chopped
1 medium potato, diced
1½ tablespoons butter
4 cups chicken stock or canned broth
Salt and pepper to taste
2 cups milk
1 tablespoon heavy cream, per serving
Nutmeg

Sauté onions, celery and potatoes in the butter until soft and translucent (cover the pan with lid to keep moisture in). Add vegetables and seasonings to stock and simmer for 30 minutes. Add milk and gently reheat. Serve with heavy cream floating on top. Add a dash of nutmeg to top of cream.

Mary Bourke's Lamb Barley Soup

INGREDIENTS:

3 lbs. of lamb neck
2 onions, sliced
4 stalks celery, sliced
2 carrots, sliced
4 tablespoons barley, soaked in a cup of cold water for 2 hours
    and drained
2 quarts of water
Salt and pepper

Cut meat into small pieces, place in a large pot and add 2 quarts of water. Heat gradually to boiling point. Skim off fat and cook for two hours. Add vegetables at end of first hour. Skim, let cool and remove remaining fat. Reheat to boiling point, add barley and cook until barley is soft.

Annie McLoughlin's Mushroom Soup

INGREDIENTS:

1 lb. mushrooms
1 medium onion, chopped
4 tablespoons butter
4 cups of chicken stock or canned chicken broth
3 tablespoons cornstarch
Salt and pepper to taste
½ cup heavy cream

Remove stems from mushrooms and chop. Reserve caps. Place chopped stems and onions in 2 tablespoons of butter and sauté for 5 minutes without browning. Add broth and simmer for 20 minutes. Slice mushroom caps and cook in remaining butter until lightly browned. Add sliced caps and 3 tablespoons cornstarch to broth. Stir with whisk until blended. Add salt and pepper and simmer for 5 minutes. Add cream, and reheat gently.

Norah McLoughlin's Mussel Soup

INGREDIENTS:

3 lbs. of mussels or 2 packages frozen shelled mussels
4 tablespoons butter
2 leeks or onions, finely chopped
4 stalks of celery, chopped
1 potato, cooked and cubed (reserve ½ cup of cooking liquid)
4 cups milk
2 teaspoons salt
½ teaspoon pepper
¼ teaspoon nutmeg

Clean and steam open the mussels in two cups of water. Reserve liquid. Melt butter, add finely chopped leeks and celery and cook for 5 minutes without browning. Stir in cubed potato and ½ cup of reserved potato water. Scald milk, add to other ingredients. Add pepper, salt and nutmeg and simmer for 20 minutes. Add 2 cups of reserved mussel liquid and then add mussels. Reheat before serving.

Pea Soup Ballintubber

INGREDIENTS:

1 cup dried peas
2 medium onions, sliced
1 large potato, diced
4 tablespoons butter or margarine
4 cups chicken stock or canned broth
½ teaspoon thyme
¼ teaspoon sage
1 bay leaf
Salt and pepper to taste
Ground mace

Rinse peas, cover with water, boil for two minutes. Remove from heat, soak for one hour. Drain.

Sauté the onions and potatoes in butter until soft. Add peas, onions and potatoes to chicken stock. Add seasonings. Cook gently until peas are tender. Seive or puree with blender or food processor and then reheat. Add a dash of mace before serving.

Katie Mangan's Potato Leek Soup

INGREDIENTS:

6 medium potatoes
3 leeks
1 medium onion, chopped
4 tablespoons butter
½ teaspoon mace
Salt and pepper to taste
6 cups chicken stock or canned broth
1 cup light cream
Chopped watercress or chives

Peel and slice potatoes. Chop onion and leeks. Cook potatoes, leeks and onions in butter, but do not brown. Add vegetables and seasonings to stock. Cover and cook slowly until vegetables are tender, about 40 minutes. Puree until smooth in blender or processor. Add cream and reheat (do not allow to boil).

Serve garnished with finely chopped watercress or chives.

Loch Conn Watercress Soup

INGREDIENTS:

1 potato, peeled and sliced
4 tablespoons butter
2 bunches coarsely chopped watercress
1 tablespoon lemon juice
4 cups chicken stock or canned broth
Salt and pepper
1 cup light cream

Sauté potato in butter until translucent. Add watercress, potato, lemon juice, salt and pepper to stock and cook for 20 minutes. Purée until smooth in blender or processor. Add cream and gently reheat.

Annie's Vegetable Soup

INGREDIENTS:

4 tablespoons butter
1 potato, diced
2 carrots, diced
1 small turnip, diced
2 stalks of celery with leaves, diced
½ cup diced onion or leek
½ cup peas, fresh or frozen
1 tomato, diced
6 cups beef stock or bouillon
Salt and pepper to taste
1 tablespoon chopped parsley

Melt butter. Sauté potatoes, carrots, turnip, celery and onion, covered, until soft and translucent (about 10 minutes).

Add peas, diced tomato and seasonings to stock. Stir in sautéed vegetables. Simmer for about 45 minutes. Garnish with chopped parsley.

Saint Patrick's Soup

INGREDIENTS:

4 tablespoons butter or margarine
1 cup raw diced potatoes
½ cup sliced onions
1 cup sliced mushrooms
1 pound spinach
4 cups chicken stock or bouillon
¼ teaspoon ground cloves
½ cup Irish oatmeal
Salt and pepper to taste
Heavy cream

Melt butter over a low heat. Add diced potatoes, sliced onions and mushrooms. Cover skillet and sauté vegetables for 8-10 minutes until soft and translucent.

Wash spinach, pick off tough stems and chop finely.

Add potatoes, onions, mushrooms and spinach to stock. Season with salt and pepper and ¼ teaspoon ground cloves. Add ½ cup Irish oatmeal. Simmer for 20 minutes.

Serve with heavy cream floating on top

Eileen's Carrot Soup

INGREDIENTS:

1 lb. carrots
1 medium onion
4 tablespoons butter
½ teaspoon salt
¼ teaspoon pepper
1 medium potato, peeled and chopped
6 cups chicken stock or canned broth
Chopped chives

Peel and shred carrots. Chop onions. Cook carrots and onions, covered, in butter for 10 minutes until the vegetables are soft. Add carrots, onions, seasonings and chopped potatoes to the stock. Simmer until vegetables are tender. Purée until smooth in blender or processor. Reheat and serve garnished with chopped chives.

Nora's Fisherman's Soup

INGREDIENTS:

1½ lbs. firm white fish (cod, scrod, sea bass) cut into 2-inch pieces
6 cups water or fish stock
2 bay leaves
1 leek or onion, chopped
2 stalks celery, chopped
2 potatoes, diced
3 tablespoons butter
3 tomatoes, chopped
½ cup chopped parsley
Celery tops, chopped
½ teaspoon thyme
Salt and pepper to taste

Place approximately ½ lb. of fish in saucepan. Cover with 6 cups of water, add bay leaf, and simmer for 15 minutes.

Sauté onions, celery and diced potatoes in 3 tablespoons of butter.

Add remaining fish, sautéed vegetables, chopped tomatoes, parsley, celery tops, thyme and salt and pepper to the stock. Add bayleaf.

Cover and simmer for 30 minutes.

Serve with brown bread.

FISH

Nancy McSpiritt's Baked Fish with Cream and Onions

INGREDIENTS:

2 lbs. white fish fillets (cod, sole, hake or haddock)
1 large onion, thinly sliced
4 tablespoons melted butter
1 teaspoon dry mustard
1 teaspoon pepper
½ teaspoon dried tarragon
½ cup cream
½ cup milk

Arrange fish fillets in buttered shallow baking dish. Place onion slices over fish. Add dry ingredients to melted butter and blend well. Pour over fish, add cream and milk.

Bake at 350° for 25 minutes or until fish flakes readily.

Bantry Bay Baked Fish with Prawn Stuffing

INGREDIENTS:

2 tablespoons melted butter
4 slices toasted white bread, crumbed
2 tablespoons water
Salt and pepper to taste
1 teaspoon chopped chives
1 teaspoon chopped parsley
½ lb. small shrimp, cooked, peeled and deveined
1½ lbs. filleted hake or white fish
Lemon slices
Sprigs of parsley

Melt butter and add to bread crumbs with water, seasonings, chives and parsley. Mix well and fold in shrimp. Spread mixture over fillets and roll. Fasten with toothpick. Place in buttered shallow baking dish. Bake in oven at 350° for 30 minutes. Garnish with parsley and lemon slices.

Mary MacNeely's Steamed Salmon Pudding with Parsley Sauce

INGREDIENTS:

     1 15½-oz. can of salmon, with reserved liquid
     1 egg, lightly beaten
     1 cup of bread crumbs or 4 slices of white bread, crumbed
     4 scallions, chopped (tops included)
     1 tablespoon chopped parsley
     Salt and pepper to taste
     ½ teaspoon vinegar
     Parsley sauce:
          2 tablespoons butter
          2 tablespoons flour
          ½ teaspoon salt
          Pepper to taste
          1 cup milk
          2 tablespoons chopped parsley
          2 sliced hard-cooked eggs

Drain salmon and reserve liquid. Beat eggs lightly, stir into the reserved liquid and add vinegar. Bone salmon. Mix bread crumbs, salmon, scallions, parsley, seasonings and vinegar into liquid. Blend well with fork.

Butter inside of pudding bowl or mold. Place ingredients in buttered bowl. Cover tightly with wax paper or foil and tie with a string. Place on a trivet in a large kettle. Add enough boiling water to come halfway up sides. Steam, covered, for 1 hour.

SAUCE: Melt butter over low heat and add flour, stirring until well blended. Stir in the milk slowly; add seasonings. Stir with whisk or wooden spoon until sauce has thickened and is smooth and hot. Fold in parsley.

TO SERVE: Place salmon pudding on serving dish and cover with parsley sauce. Garnish with sliced hard-cooked egg.

Laura Rudman's Fish Au Gratin

INGREDIENTS:

2 cups milk
1 small chopped onion
1 cup sliced mushrooms
1 diced carrot
1 stalk celery, diced
2 cloves
1 bay leaf
Salt and pepper to taste
4 tablespoons butter
4 tablespoons flour
4 ounces diced cheese, Cheddar or Blarney
1½ lbs. white fish fillets
4 potatoes, cooked and mashed
1 tablespoon butter

Place one cup of milk, vegetables and seasonings in a saucepan. Bring to boil, cover and cook for 20 minutes. Add butter, flour and one cup of milk. Stir until sauce thickens. Add cheese. Stir over low heat until cheese melts.

Place fish in shallow dish or oven-proof platter. Bake for 15 minutes at 350°. Add sauce and bake for 10 minutes or until fish flakes.

Using fluted pastry tube, ruffle a border of potatoes around edge of baking dish. Brush potatoes with melted butter and place under broiler until lightly browned.

Kerry Broiled Fish with Emerald Butter

INGREDIENTS:

2 lbs. cod, haddock or any white fish, filleted
½ cup butter or oil
⅓ cup chopped parsley
½ cup chopped dill
1 scallion, chopped
Juice of 1 lemon

Brush fish lightly on each side with melted butter or oil. Place on hot pan in broiler, about two inches from the heat. Broil until the flesh is clear white and flakes easily, about 10-15 minutes, depending upon the thickness of fillets. Remove to warmed serving dish

Melt butter. Blend in the parsley, dill, scallion and lemon juice and pour over the fillets.

Aran Island's Fisherman's Pie

INGREDIENTS:

1½ lbs. of cooked flaked fish (scrod, cod, hake or smoked fish)
3 tablespoons butter
1 onion, finely chopped
4 tablespoons flour
1 tablespoon mild mustard
1½ cups milk
½ cup fish stock
½ cup mushrooms or 4 oz. can
2 tablespoons chopped parsley
½ teaspoon mace
2 hard cooked eggs, chopped
For the pastry:
½ cup margarine or butter
1 tablespoon water
1½ cups flour, sifted

Heat butter in saucepan, add onion and cook for three minutes. Stir in flour and mustard. Blend in milk and fish stock and stir until thickened. Add flaked fish, mushrooms, parsley, mace and chopped eggs to the sauce and blend. Place in 9 inch pie dish and cover with crust.

FOR THE CRUST: Place margarine, water and half the flour in mixing bowl and cream with fork until well mixed. Stir in remaining flour to make a firm dough. Place on a lightly floured board and knead until smooth. Roll into a circle, fold and cut several gashes in top. Unfold carefully over pie filling.

Bake at 425° for 35-40 minutes.

Bridget's Fish in a Parcel

INGREDIENTS:

2 lbs. fish fillets (haddock, hake, cod, scrod)
1 cup freshly made bread crumbs
2 tablespoons chopped parsley
Juice and grated rind of 1 lemon
2 tablespoons butter, melted
½ onion, minced
Salt and pepper to taste
2 tablespoons melted butter
Lemon slices
Parsley sprigs

Clean and trim fish. Slit fish with sharp knife to make a pocket.

Mix bread crumbs, parsley and grated lemon rind. Melt butter and sauté onion gently. Pour over bread crumbs and blend. Season to taste. (Add 1 or 2 tablespoons of boiling water if moister dressing is desired).

Fill pocket with dressing. Sprinkle with lemon juice and brush tops with melted butter.

Cut oval shaped pieces of foil, large enough for each serving, and brush with oil or butter. Lay stuffed fish on foil. Wrap loosely and bake at 400° for 30-45 minutes.

Serve in foil with edges rolled back to form boat shaped opening. Garnish with lemon slices and parsley sprigs.

Noreen Heffernan's Grilled Salmon Steaks

INGREDIENTS:

4 salmon steaks
2 tablespoons melted butter
Lemon and mustard butter:
    4 tablespoons butter, room temperature
    4 tablespoons lemon juice
    1 teaspoon dry mustard
    Salt and pepper
    Broiled tomato halves
    Parsley

Preheat broiler. Brush salmon steaks with melted butter. Place on broiler, turning after 5 minutes. Continue broiling for 5 more minutes.

For lemon butter: Cream butter and mix in lemon juice, dry mustard, salt and pepper. Stir until well blended.

TO SERVE: Arrange on serving dish and top with lemon and mustard butter. Garnish with parsley and broiled tomato halves.

St. Brendan's Baked Scallops
INGREDIENTS:
1½ lbs. scallops
1 cup fish stock or clam juice
3 tablespoons butter
3 tablespoons flour
1 cup milk
4 tablespoons chopped chives
3 tablespoons dry white wine or lemon juice
⅛ teaspoon dry mustard
Salt and pepper to taste
1 cup freshly made bread crumbs
1 tablespoon butter
Lemon slices
Parsley

Grease 6 scallop shells or ramekins

Poach scallops in stock for 3 minutes. Drain, reserving stock. Place scallops in shells. (If scallops are large, chop coarsely.)

Melt butter, stir in flour and cook for 4-5 minutes without browning. Stir in milk and fish stock and cook for 7 minutes. Season with dry mustard, salt and pepper. Add wine or juice and blend.

Pour over scallops in shells. Sprinkle with bread crumbs and dot with butter.

Bake for 10-15 minutes at 400°, until browned.

Garnish with lemon and parsley.

Clew Bay Scallops

INGREDIENTS:

1 pound scallops
8 tablespoons flour
1 teaspoon baking powder
Salt and pepper
¾ cup milk
Cooking oil
Lemon wedges
Parsley

Mix 4 tablespoons flour, 1 teaspoon baking powder, and seasonings. Add milk and stir until the batter is smooth. Coat scallops with remaining flour and dip into the batter.

Heat oil in skillet. Fry scallops until batter is golden brown. Drain well on paper towel. Serve garnished with parsley and lemon wedges.

Serving suggestions: Serve with boiled new potatoes and West Country peas. (p. 61)

Fish Fried in Oatmeal

INGREDIENTS:

1½ lbs. fish fillets
¾ cup of flour
1 egg
2 tablespoons milk
1½ cups of Irish oatmeal or quick-oats
Salt and pepper to taste
6 tablespoons of oil
Lemon wedges

Pat fish dry with paper towels.
Beat egg lightly and add 2 tablespoons of milk.
Add salt and pepper to the flour.
Dip fish first in seasoned flour and then in beaten egg. Roll in oatmeal until thoroughly coated.
Heat oil in large skillet. Fry fish on both sides until crisp.
Garnish with lemon wedges.

Bay Prawns in Sauce

INGREDIENTS:

3 tablespoons butter
3 tablespoons flour
1½ cups milk
2 tablespoons lemon juice
1 scallion, chopped
1 bay leaf
½ pound small shrimp, cooked and peeled
Salt and pepper to taste
1 hard-cooked egg, grated

Melt butter in saucepan, stir in the flour and cook for 2 to 3 minutes. Add the milk gradually, stirring continuously. Bring to a boil and simmer for 5 minutes, stirring constantly. Add lemon juice, scallion and bay leaf and simmer for 3 minutes. Fold in shrimp and reheat.

Serve on toast slices and garnish with grated egg.

MEAT

Kitty Brady's Boiled Beef with Horseradish Sauce

INGREDIENTS:

3 pounds fresh brisket of beef
3 onions, sliced
2 stalks celery, chopped coarsely
2 bay leaves
2 sprigs parsley
1 teaspoon thyme
1 teaspoon black pepper
1 teaspoon salt
3 cups water
4 carrots, sliced
4 white turnips, quartered
For the sauce:
    ½ cup heavy cream
    ½ cup sour cream
    3 tablespoons prepared horseradish
    ½ teaspoon salt

Place beef in dutch oven, add onions, celery, bay leaves, parsley, thyme, pepper and salt. Add three cups of water or enough to cover the beef. Cover and simmer for 1½ hours. Add sliced carrots and turnips and continue to cook for ½ hour, or until the meat is tender when pierced with a fork. Remove beef, slice and arrange on heated platter surrounded by vegetables. Serve sauce separately.

FOR THE SAUCE: Whip ½ cup of heavy cream and fold in the sour cream. Add 3 tablespoons of prepared horseradish and ½ teaspoon salt and mix well.

Beef Stew with Guinness and Prunes

INGREDIENTS:

2 lbs. lean stewing beef
2 tablespoons flour
1½ teaspoons salt
Pepper to taste
2 tablespoons cooking oil
2 small sliced onions
2 bay leaves
½ cup Guinness stout
½ cup water
4 medium carrots, thinly sliced
1 cup pitted prunes, soaked and drained

Cut beef into serving pieces. Mix flour, salt and pepper. Dredge the beef in the seasoned flour. Brown the meat on all sides in the cooking oil. Add bay leaves and onions and continue cooking until lightly browned. Place in dutch oven or casserole and add Guinness and water. (If necessary, add more water to cover meat.) Add sliced carrots. Cover and bake for 40 minutes at 350°. Add prunes and continue cooking for ½ hour.

Serve with parsleyed potatoes.

Lily's Beltra Baked Cottage Ham

INGREDIENTS:

1½-2 pound cottage ham (smoked shoulder butt)
10 whole cloves
1 cup cider or apple juice
3 tablespoons honey
2 small apples, peeled and diced

Preheat oven to 325°.

Cut diagonal gashes on the top of ham and insert cloves. Mix honey and cider and stir in apples. Place ham in ovenproof casserole and spoon cider mixture over it. Cover and bake for 1 hour and 15 minutes.

Serve with braised cabbage (p. 58) and baked potatoes.

Mixed Grill Ennis

INGREDIENTS:

8 breakfast sausages
8 strips of Irish or thickly sliced bacon
4 lamb chops
4 tomatoes, halved
16 large mushroom caps
2 tablespoons butter
Salt and pepper

Preheat broiler.
Place sausages in 1½ cups of boiling water and boil for 5 minutes to remove fat. Drain well. Wash and remove stems from mushrooms. Brush tomatoes and mushrooms with butter, add salt and pepper. Place lamb chops, sausages and bacon on broiler rack and broil for 7 minutes. Turn meat and add tomatoes and mushrooms. Continue broiling for 7 minutes.
Serve with french fried potatoes.

Bridget Madden's Kidney Stew

INGREDIENTS:

6 lamb kidneys
1 chopped onion
2 stalks chopped celery
1 tablespoon Worcestershire sauce
½ teaspoon Kitchen Bouquet
2 tablespoons cooking oil
Salt and pepper to taste

Cut kidneys in half and remove membrane. After membrane is removed, cut into small pieces. Sauté kidneys quickly in the oil until they lose red color.
Add onions and celery, cook briefly, stirring until onions are translucent. Add Worcestershire sauce, Kitchen Bouquet and then add water to cover; simmer for 25 to 30 minutes. If sauce is too thin, thicken with flour.
Serve with mashed potatoes or rice.

Catherine Kelleher's Lamb and Beef Stew

INGREDIENTS:

1 large onion, chopped
2 tablespoons vegetable oil
½ lb. lamb necks
1½ lbs. stewing beef
1½ tablespoons flour
2 cups bouillon or stock
6 carrots, quartered
3 stalks celery, chopped
1 bay leaf
Salt and pepper to taste
6 potatoes, peeled and quartered

Preheat oven to 300°.

Brown onions in vegetable oil. Add lamb and beef and continue browning. Pour off fat. Sprinkle with flour and cook a few minutes longer. Remove meat to dutch oven or large casserole and add bouillon or stock. Add carrots, celery and seasonings. Cover and place in oven. Bake at 300° for 1 hour. Add potatoes and cook for 1 hour longer.

Theresa Reape's Lamb Steaks

INGREDIENTS:

4 carrots
4 potatoes
3 parsnips
4 lamb steaks
Salt and pepper

Peel and slice carrots, potatoes and parsnips. Cook vegetables in boiling water for 10 minutes in a covered saucepan. Drain and reserve cooking liquid.

Brown the lamb steaks in heavy skillet. Add vegetables and liquid to steaks. Season with salt and pepper to taste. Cook for 20 minutes at medium heat or until meat and vegetables are tender.

Nancy McSpiritt's Lamb Pie

INGREDIENTS:

> 2 cups cooked lamb, cubed
> 3 stalks celery, finely chopped
> 4 carrots, thinly sliced
> 1 onion, thinly sliced
> Salt and pepper to taste
> 1 cup gravy or thickened stock
> Short-crust pastry:
>> 1 cup flour
>> ½ cup butter
>> ¼ teaspoon salt
>> 3-4 tablespoons ice water

Preheat oven to 425°.

Cut meat into small cubes, add seasonings, vegetables and gravy. Place in 9 inch pie dish. Top with pastry. Bake at 425° for 25-30 minutes.

PASTRY: In bowl, mix flour and salt. With pastry blender, cut in butter until mixture resembles coarse grain. Sprinkle water over flour mixture and mix lightly with a fork. Use only enough water so that pastry will hold together when pressed gently into a ball. Roll out pastry and cover the pie dish.

Roast Leg of Lamb Connemara

INGREDIENTS:

> 1 leg of lamb (5-6 lbs.)
> 1 clove of garlic, peeled
> Juice of ½ lemon
> 1 tablespoon rosemary

Preheat oven to 350°.

Rub the leg with garlic clove. Using a pastry brush paint the leg with a mixture of lemon juice and rosemary.

Place the meat, fat side up, on a rack in an uncovered roasting pan. Immediately after placing lamb in oven reduce heat to 325°. Do not cover or baste. Roast it 30 minutes to the pound. Serve with mint sauce.

Mint Sauce:

INGREDIENTS:

½ cup cider vinegar
1 tablespoon sugar
¼ teaspoon salt
½ cup finely chopped mint

Put vinegar, sugar and salt in small saucepan. Heat until boiling and sugar is dissolved. Pour mixture over the mint and let stand 1 hour.

Before serving reheat over a low flame.

Mary Hanley's Lamb Stew

INGREDIENTS:

3 lbs. neck of lamb or 1 lb. neck of lamb and 2 lbs. shoulder
blade and bone lamb chops
3 medium onions
8 medium potatoes
Salt and pepper to taste
1 teaspoon thyme
2 cups water
3 tablespoons chopped parsley

Preheat oven to 350°.

Trim excess fat from meat and cut into cubes. Peel and slice the onions. Peel the potatoes and thinly slice two of them. Cut remaining potatoes into quarters. Arrange a layer of sliced potatoes on bottom of greased dutch oven or casserole. Cover with a layer of lamb, then a layer of onions. Add seasonings and cover with quartered potatoes. Add two cups of water. Cover the casserole and cook in a 350° oven for 1½ hours or until the lamb is tender.

Remove from oven and sprinkle with chopped parsley.

Angela's Stuffed Pork Chops

INGREDIENTS:

4 rib or loin pork chops, 1½ inch thick
3 tablespoons margarine or butter
For the stuffing:
1 cup freshly made bread crumbs
2 tablespoons butter
¼ cup raisins
1 egg, beaten
Salt and pepper to taste
1½-2 lbs. yellow turnips or rutabagas
Chopped parsley

Preheat oven to 325°.
Cut a pocket through lean part to the bone of each chop.
FOR THE STUFFING: Melt 2 tablespoons butter, add bread crumbs and raisins and blend well. Add beaten egg to bread crumbs and mix. Season with salt and pepper.
Stuff the chops with the dressing.
Melt 3 tablespoons margarine in skillet. Brown the chops.
Peel and slice turnips and layer on bottom of casserole. Place chops on top of turnips. Add ½ cup of boiling water and sprinkle with chopped parsley. Cover tightly. Bake at 325° for 1½ hours.

Mary Moffat's Spare Ribs and Cabbage

INGREDIENTS:

4 lbs. spareribs (allow one pound per serving)
1 medium cabbage
Salt and pepper to taste
1 teaspoon caraway seeds (optional)

Place spareribs in water to cover. Add seasonings and caraway seeds. Bring to a boil and simmer for 1½ to 2 hours.
Cut cabbage into sixths. 20 minutes before ribs are completed, place cabbage wedges on top of spareribs. Cover with lid. Cook until cabbage is just tender, about 20 minutes.
Remove cabbage with slotted spoon and drain. Remove spareribs with slotted spoon and place on a warm platter. Arrange cabbage around the ribs. Serve with potatoes in jacket or parsleyed potatoes.

Ardagh Pork, Potato and Apple Stew

INGREDIENTS:

6 pork chops
6 medium potatoes
4 cooking apples
3 medium onions
Salt and pepper to taste
2 tablespoons brown sugar
¼ teaspoon nutmeg
¼ teaspoon cinnamon
⅛ teaspoon ginger

Preheat oven to 350°.

Trim fat from pork chops and set aside. Peel potatoes and onions and slice. Peel, core and slice apples.

In large casserole, layer half the potatoes, onions and apples. Sprinkle with salt, pepper and one tablespoon of brown sugar. Add chops in a single layer. Cover with remaining potatoes, onions and apples. Sprinkle with remaining sugar and spices.

Cover and bake at 350° for 1½ hours or until meat is tender.

Thurles Baked Liver and Bacon

INGREDIENTS:

1 lb. calf's liver
1 cup freshly made bread crumbs
1 teaspoon chopped parsley
Salt and pepper to taste
2 tablespoons butter or margarine, melted
1 tablespoon chopped onion
3 slices bacon, cut in half
¼ cup stock or chicken bouillon
1 bay leaf

Cut liver into strips about 1 inch thick and place in casserole.

Mix breadcrumbs, parsley, chopped onion, butter and seasonings. Spread a little on each slice of liver. Cut bacon slices in half and place on top of stuffing. Add bay leaf to stock and pour into casserole.

Cover with foil. Bake at 400° for 30 minutes.

Boiled Ham and Cabbage

INGREDIENTS:

½ ham (about 6 lbs.)
2 cups gingerale or cider
1½ quarts of water
2 bay leaves
4 whole cloves
1 medium sliced onion
1 medium cabbage

Place the ham in a large pot and cover with gingerale and water. Bring to a boil and then reduce heat. Simmer for 1½ to 2 hours until tender.

Cut cabbage into 6 pieces. 20 minutes before ham is cooked place cabbage wedges on top of ham. Cover with lid. Cook until cabbage is just tender (about 20 minutes).

Remove cabbage, drain and keep warm. Let ham cool in the stock for 20 minutes before serving.

To serve: Place sliced ham on a warm platter. Surround with cabbage wedges and boiled potatoes.

Josie's Shepherd's Pie

INGREDIENTS:

2 lbs. ground beef
1 tablespoon oil
2 onions, finely chopped
2 tomatoes, chopped
1 cup beef stock or bouillon
½ teaspoon thyme
¼ teaspoon sage
1 tablespoon chopped parsley
Salt and pepper to taste
5 medium potatoes, boiled and mashed
1 tablespoon butter

Preheat oven to 375°.

Brown beef in oil. Remove from pan and set aside. Drain most of accumulated fat from pan. Sauté onions until tender, add chopped tomatoes and cook for 2-3 minutes. Add broth and stir in herbs and seasonings. Return browned meat to skillet and continue cooking for 5 minutes.

Transfer all ingredients to a casserole or deep 9-inch pie dish. Top with mashed potatoes, scoring them with fork. Dot with butter and bake uncovered in 375° oven for 35-40 minutes.

Emily's Roast Beef with Roast Vegetables

INGREDIENTS:

1 standing rib roast, 5-6 lbs.
2 tablespoons prepared mustard
Potatoes, peeled
Carrots, peeled and halved
Parsnips, peeled and quartered
Onions, peeled
Parsley

Spread mustard over roast. Place roast, fat side up, in roasting pan on a rack. Roast beef at 450° for 15 minutes. Lower heat to 350° and roast until cooked to taste, basting occasionally. Allow 18 minutes per pound for rare, 25 minutes per pound for medium and 30 minutes per pound for well done beef.

Prepare vegetables. Parboil potatoes for 10 minutes. Drain well. Place all vegetables around meat 50 minutes before roasting is completed.

Remove roast from oven, carve and place on heated serving dish, arrange vegetables around the roast. Garnish with parsley

Stuffed Pork Fillets (Pork Tenderloin) Traditional

INGREDIENTS:

3 medium pork tenderloins
2 tablespoons butter
Salt and pepper
For the stuffing:
    1 onion
    2 tablespoons butter
    2 cups white breadcrumbs, freshly made
    ½ cup chopped parsley
    ½ teaspoon poultry seasoning
    Salt and pepper
    1 egg, beaten

Preheat oven to 350°.

Split the tenderloins carefully down the center without cutting in half, forming a pocket to contain the stuffing. Sandwich the filling into the tenderloin, draw the edges together and tie securely with string. Rub with butter and season with salt and pepper. Place on rack in roasting pan and cover with foil. Cook for 1¼ hours.

Not traditional but very tasty: cover with sliced apples or sliced onions while roasting.

STUFFING: Chop the onion and brown lightly in 1 tablespoon butter. Combine with breadcrumbs, parsley, seasonings and remaining butter. Add the beaten egg and mix well.

POULTRY

Theresa McGowan's Chicken and Cucumber

INGREDIENTS:

¼ lb. sliced bacon
4 tablespoons butter
3 onions
1 pound mushrooms
1 large cucumber
4 chicken breasts, skinned and boned
4 tablespoons flour
1 cup stock or bouillon
½ cup heavy cream .
½ cup white wine (optional)
Parsley

Cook bacon until crisp, crumble and set aside. Peel and slice onions and cucumber. Trim and slice mushrooms. Place two tablespoons butter in pan and sauté onions, mushrooms, and cucumber until brown, stirring occasionally. Set aside.

Melt two tablespoons butter in pan and add boned chicken; cook for 15 minutes. Sprinkle with flour and gradually blend in stock and cream. Add mushrooms, onions, and cucumber and cook slowly for 5 minutes until warm.

Place on serving dish and sprinkle with crumbled bacon and chopped parsley.

Serve with rice.

Kitty's Chicken

INGREDIENTS:

1 frying chicken, about 3½ lbs., cut into serving pieces
¾ cup flour
Salt and pepper to taste
4-6 tablespoons butter
1 cup chicken bouillon or stock
2 teaspoons tarragon
2 chopped scallions
Chopped parsley

Mix flour with salt and pepper. Dredge the chicken in flour mixture. Brown the chicken pieces in butter in heavy skillet.

When browned on all sides, add bouillon, tarragon and chopped scallions. Lower the heat, cover and cook until chicken is tender, 35 to 45 minutes.

Remove chicken to warm serving dish. Pour sauce over chicken. Garnish with chopped parsley.

Saint Stephen's Day Casserole
December 26

INGREDIENTS:

- 3 tablespoons butter
- 1 onion, finely chopped
- 4 tablespoons flour
- 1 tablespoon mild mustard
- 1½ cups chicken stock
- ½ cup heavy cream
- 2 cups of cubed cooked chicken or turkey
- 1 cup of cubed cooked ham
- ½ cup mushrooms or 4-ounce can
- 2 tablespoons chopped parsley
- 1 teaspoon minced rosemary
- 1 frozen puff pastry or short-crust pastry (p. 54)

Heat butter in saucepan. Add the onions and cook for 3 minutes. Stir in the flour and mustard and cook briefly. Blend in chicken stock and cream and stir until thickened. Add cubed chicken and ham, mushrooms, parsley and rosemary to the sauce.

Place in 9-inch pie dish, cover with crust or frozen puff pastry.

Bake at 425° for 25–30 minutes.

Christmas Roast Goose with Nephin Stuffing

INGREDIENTS:

> 1 10 lb. goose (allow 1 lb. per serving)
> 1 apple
> For the stuffing:
>> 6 medium potatoes
>> 3 tablespoons butter
>> ½ cup warm milk
>> 8 scallions, finely chopped
>> 1 cup raisins

Preheat oven to 400°

Wash and dry the goose. Rub inside lightly with salt. Cook and mash potatoes. Add butter, warm milk and seasonings. Beat until smooth. Add raisins and scallions and mix well. Wrap the stuffing in foil.

Insert apple and wrappped stuffing into cavity. Place the goose on a rack in an uncovered roasting pan, breast side up. Prick skin lightly with a fork to release fat.

Roast at 400° for thirty minutes then reduce heat to 350°. Allow 20 minutes per pound and 20 minutes extra.

Serve with warm applesauce flavored with rind of one orange.

Mary's Chicken Stew

INGREDIENTS:

> 1 3½ lb. chicken, cut into serving pieces
> ¾ cup flour
> Salt and pepper to taste
> 5 slices bacon
> 6 small onions, peeled
> 4 carrots, quartered
> 1 small turnip, thinly sliced
> 6 small potatoes, peeled
> 2 cups chicken broth
> ½ teaspoon sage

Season flour with salt and pepper. Dredge chicken in seasoned flour. Fry bacon in large skillet, remove and reserve.

Place chicken in skillet and brown on all sides. Transfer to large casserole or Dutch oven. Add onions, carrots, turnips and potatoes. Cover with chicken broth. Sprinkle with sage and crumbled bacon.

Cover casserole and bake at 350° for one hour or until chicken and vegetables are tender.

Catherine's Poached Chicken

INGREDIENTS:

1 3 lb. chicken, quartered, or 3 whole chicken breasts, halved
½ orange
1 cup chopped carrots
1 cup chopped celery
½ teaspoon thyme
2 tablespoons minced onions
½ teaspoon white pepper
For the sauce:
    4 tablespoons butter
    4 tablespoons flour
    2½ cups chicken stock
    3-4 tablespoons cream
    Chopped parsley

Rub the chicken with orange.

Place the chicken in a large saucepan or Dutch oven. Barely cover with boiling water. Add the vegetables and seasonings. Cover and simmer gently until chicken is tender, approximately 45 minutes.

Remove chicken and vegetables from stock and reserve. Keep vegetables warm.

FOR THE SAUCE: Melt butter in saucepan and stir in the flour. Cook for a few minutes, stirring. Add chicken stock and bring to a boil, stirring constantly. Reduce heat and simmer for 15 minutes, stirring occasionally.

Remove skin from chicken and cut chicken into large serving pieces.

Place chicken in sauce and heat gently for 10 minutes.

Serve on a bed of hot rice, topped with reserved vegetables. Garnish with parsley.

Chicken with Ham
(chicken and ham are traditionally served together)

INGREDIENTS:

1 chicken (about 3½ pounds)
1½-2 pound cottage ham (pork butt)
12 cloves
Stuffing:
    8 slices of white bread (crust removed)
    ½ cup milk
    4 tablespoons chopped parsley
    1 chicken liver (sautéed and chopped)
    1 small onion, chopped
    ¼ teaspoon mace
    Salt and pepper to taste

Wash, dry and salt the chicken inside and out. Soak the bread in the milk, add finely chopped parsley, chicken liver and onion, mace, salt and pepper. Mix with a fork. Place stuffing in the cavity. Score the ham and insert cloves. Place chicken and ham on rack in roasting pan. Cook in a 350° oven for 1½ hours, or until both are tender and golden brown.

HIGH TEA

Marian's Bacon Tart
(modern variation of a traditional recipe)
INGREDIENTS:
For the filling:

6 slices bacon

2 cups sliced mushrooms

6 scallions

1 lb. cottage cheese, uncreamed

2 eggs, separated

½ teaspoon *fines herbes*

Salt and pepper to taste

For the pastry:

1½ cups flour

1 teaspoon salt

4 tablespoons butter

4 tablespoons cold water (approximately)

FOR THE PASTRY: Mix flour and salt. Cut butter into flour with pastry blender until it resembles meal. Sprinkle dough with 4 tablespoons cold water and blend lightly with a fork. Shape into a ball and refrigerate.

FOR THE FILLING: Dice and fry bacon, drain and set aside. Slice mushrooms and scallions and sauté lightly. Separate two eggs. Beat yolks lightly with a fork and add to cottage cheese. Add *fines herbes,* salt and pepper and blend. Add bacon, mushrooms and scallions and mix well. Beat egg whites until stiff and fold into mixture.

Roll out pastry to fit a 9-inch pie tin. Put filling into the pastry shell. Bake in a moderate oven at 350° until cooked and set (about 50 minutes).

Peggy's Eggs in a Nest
INGREDIENTS:

6 medium potatoes

4 tablespoons butter

⅓ cup warmed milk

Salt and pepper to taste

4 eggs

Preheat oven to 350°.

Peel and cook potatoes in boiling salted water until soft. Drain, then mash with fork or masher. Add butter and warm milk and beat until smooth. Season with salt and pepper to taste.

Shape potatoes into four nests, making a hollow with spoon to contain the egg. Place nests on greased baking sheet and break an egg into each nest. Bake at 350° for 8 to 10 minutes. Centers should be soft and the whites set.

Serve with Irish bacon and sausages.

Irene's Cheese Pudding

INGREDIENTS:

2 cups milk
2 tablespoons butter
¼ teaspoon prepared mustard
Salt and pepper to taste
3 eggs, separated
½ cup freshly made breadcrumbs
½ cup grated cheese
1 tomato, sliced

Preheat oven to 375°.

Heat milk and butter in saucepan. Separate three eggs. Beat yolks lightly with a fork, then add to the heated milk. Add mustard, salt and pepper and blend well.

Mix breadcrumbs and cheese. Reserve one tablespoon for topping. Pour heated milk mixture over breadcrumbs and allow to stand for 30 minutes.

Beat egg whites until stiff and fold into cooled mixture.

Butter an oven proof dish and fill with mixture. Top with 1 tablespoon of reserved cheese.

Bake at 375° for 20-25 minutes until lightly browned.

Remove from oven and place a row of sliced tomatoes down the center of pudding. Return to oven and bake for 5 minutes.

Bridget Paton's Summer Crab Salad

INGREDIENTS:

1 cup cooked crab meat, picked over
3 cups cooked rice
¼ cup mayonnaise
½ cup heavy cream
Salt and pepper to taste
1 scallion, chopped finely
1 teaspoon dried tarragon
2 hard-cooked eggs, sieved
Watercress

Combine crab meat and rice. Blend mayonnaise, cream, seasonings, tarragon and scallion. Add to rice mixture and fold in gently. Place on serving dish and garnish with watercress and sieved hard-cooked eggs.

Serve with thinly sliced whole-grain bread (p. 73).

Blarney Cheese Delight

INGREDIENTS:

6 thin slices Blarney cheese
4 slices white bread
1 cup milk
2 eggs
½ teaspoon salt
¼ teaspoon pepper

Place sliced cheese between bread slices making 2 sandwiches of 3 slices of cheese apiece. Beat milk, eggs, salt and pepper with fork. Dip sandwiches into batter and cook on a hot griddle, turning once, until nicely browned.

Serve with sliced tomatoes.

VARIATION: Thin slices of ham or cooked bacon may be inserted in the sandwich before dipping into batter.

VEGETABLES

Laura Rudman's Brussels Sprouts

INGREDIENTS:

    1 lb. brussels sprouts
    2 tablespoons butter
    2 tablespoons flour
    1 teaspoon salt
    ½ teaspoon pepper
    ⅔ cup milk
    ⅓ cup of liquid, reserved from cooking sprouts
    1 hard-cooked egg, sieved

Remove wilted leaves from sprouts, trim and cut a cross in each stem. Wash thoroughly. Place in small amount of boiling water and cover. Boil rapidly for 10 to 20 minutes or until tender. Drain and keep warm, reserving ⅓ cup of cooking liquid.

Melt 2 tablespoons of butter in smalll saucepan. Stir in flour and gradually add ⅔ cup of milk and ⅓ cup of cooking liquid reserved from vegetables. Simmer over low heat, stirring continuously, until sauce is thick and smooth.

Place sprouts on serving dish and cover with sauce. Garnish with sieved hard-cooked egg.

Ellen's Braised Cabbage

INGREDIENTS:

    1 medium cabbage
    1 chopped onion
    4 slices of bacon
    2 tablespoons butter
    Salt and pepper

Quarter the cabbage and remove the core. Shred cabbage finely. Chop the bacon and onion into small pieces. Melt butter and fry bacon and onion for about 4 minutes. Add shredded cabbage, salt and pepper. Cover the pan and simmer for about 12 to 15 minutes, stirring frequently.

Eileen Kelly's Cabbage Baked in Cream

INGREDIENTS:

3 cups shredded cabbage
1 cup heavy cream
½ teaspoon nutmeg
Salt and pepper to taste

Preheat oven to 325°
Place shredded cabbage in a buttered baking dish. Add nutmeg, salt and pepper and cover with cream. Bake for 45 minutes at 325°.

Maura's Carrots and Parsnips

INGREDIENTS:

6 carrots
6 parsnips
2 tablespoons butter
½ teaspoon ground cloves
Salt and pepper
Chopped parsley

Trim and peel carrots and parsnips and slice or cube. Cook, covered, in about 2 inches of boiling water for 10 to 15 minutes or until tender. Drain well. Mash carrots and parsnips and beat in butter. Add cloves, salt and pepper and stir until smooth. Heap the mixture in a mound on a serving platter and garnish with chopped parsley.

Kathleen Mangan's Steamed Carrots Glazed with Honey

INGREDIENTS:

1½ lbs. carrots
½ cup water
⅓ cup butter
⅓ cup honey
1 teaspoon salt
Chopped parsley

Scrape the carrots and cut into ½-inch strips. Place in a vegetable steamer with ½ cup water. Cover and cook for 15 minutes. Melt butter in a saucepan, add honey and cook over a low flame for 3 minutes. Add carrots to honey mixture and stir gently to glaze. Serve sprinkled with chopped parsley.

Angela's Cheese Cauliflower

INGREDIENTS:

1 medium cauliflower
2 tablespoons flour
2 tablespoons butter
1 cup milk
½ cup grated Cheddar or Blarney cheese
Salt and pepper to taste

Wash and remove lower stalks from medium firm, crisp head of cauliflower. Break into florets. Cook until tender in boiling salted water (5 to 7 minutes). Drain well.

SAUCE: In saucepan, over low heat, melt butter. Add flour, salt and pepper and stir until well blended. Slowly add milk while stirring constantly. Cook, stirring, until smooth and thickened.

Arrange cauliflower in baking dish, cover with sauce and sprinkle with grated cheese. Bake in oven at 450° for 15 minutes or until heated thoroughly and golden on top.

Emily's Braised Celery

INGREDIENTS:

1 bunch celery
1 sliced onion
1 thinly sliced carrot
2 tablespoons butter
½ cup chicken stock or bouillon
Salt and pepper

Wash and clean celery. Remove leaves. Cut stalks into even lengths. Sauté celery, onion, and carrot in butter for about 5 minutes. Add broth, salt and pepper. Cover and cook over low heat for 15 minutes or until celery is tender.

West Country Garden Peas

INGREDIENTS:

2 cups drained, cooked fresh or frozen peas
¼ lb. mushrooms, sliced
5 scallions snipped into 1-inch pieces
2 tablespoons butter
½ teaspoon salt
¼ teaspoon pepper
¼ teaspoon nutmeg

In butter, over medium heat, sauté scallions and mushrooms until lightly browned, about 3 minutes. Stir in salt, pepper and nutmeg. Add peas and heat gently. Serve with additional butter if desired.

Scalloped Potatoes Donegal

INGREDIENTS:

6 medium potatoes, washed and thinly sliced but not peeled
2 medium sliced onions
3 tablespoons whole wheat flour
1 teaspoon salt
½ teaspoon pepper
4 tablespoons butter
2 cups milk

Preheat oven to 350°.

Arrange half of potatoes in greased baking dish. Cover with a layer of onions. Sprinkle with half of combined flour, salt and pepper and dot with butter; repeat the process. Add just enough milk so it can be seen between top slices. Cover and bake at 350° for 30 minutes; remove cover and continue baking for about 30 minutes or until tender and browned.

Traditional Champ

INGREDIENTS:

5 medium potatoes
Salt and pepper
5 tablespoons butter
8 scallions, chopped
½ cup milk

Cook potatoes in boiling salted water until soft, drain well and shake over low heat until white and floury. Mash or press through a ricer. Season with salt and pepper. Combine milk and chopped scallions in a small saucepan and cook for 3 minutes.

Add butter, milk and scallions to mashed potatoes and beat until light and fluffy.

Put into warmed serving dish, forming a mound. Make a well in the center and fill with butter.

Jacqueline Rudman's Boxty Pancakes

INGREDIENTS:

6 medium potatoes
¾ cup flour
1 teaspoon baking powder
1 teaspoon salt
2 eggs
½ cup plus 1 tablespoon milk

Wash and peel three potatoes. Place potatoes in cold, salted water, bring to a boil and cook until tender. Drain. Mash with fork or masher until all lumps have been removed. Allow to cool slightly.

Wash and peel three more potatoes and grate. Put grated potatoes into clean cloth. Squeeze cloth tightly to remove all the excess moisture. Blend into the mashed potatoes.

Sift flour, baking powder and salt into a bowl. Beat eggs with a fork. Add potatoes, eggs and ¼ cup of milk to the flour and stir. Add remaining milk and mix well to make a thick batter.

Lightly brush a griddle or electric frying pan with margarine. Heat through, then drop a spoonful of the mixture onto the hot pan, spread out slightly to form a round. Turn heat to low and cook until golden brown, turning once, about 8 minutes on each side. Remove from heat and keep warm. Repeat with remaining mixture.

Serve with lots of butter or jam.

Delicious with grilled lamb chops.

Linenhall Boxty

INGREDIENTS:

4 medium potatoes
1 onion
1 egg, lightly beaten
2 tablespoons flour
Salt and pepper to taste
4 tablespoons cooking oil

Peel and grate potatoes and onion. Add egg, flour, salt and pepper and mix well. Meantime, heat oil in heavy skillet. Drop mixture by tablespoon into skillet and spread out slightly to form a round. Fry until golden brown, turning once, about 3 to 4 minutes on each side. Repeat with remaining mixture. Serve warm with butter or jam.

Jim Kelleher's Mashed Turnips

INGREDIENTS:

    1 large yellow turnip
    1 apple, peeled and quartered
    3 tablespoons butter
    ¼ teaspoon ginger
    Salt and pepper to taste

Wash, pare and cut turnip into slices. Peel and quarter the apple. Drop turnip and apple into rapidly boiling water to cover. Add ½ teaspoon salt. Cook, uncovered, for 15 to 20 minutes or until tender. Drain well. Mash with potato masher or electric mixer until no lumps remain. Add butter, ginger and pepper and beat with spoon or mixer until smooth and creamy.

Kilcullen Creamed Turnips

INGREDIENTS:

    1 lb. turnips
    1 lb. potatoes
    4 tablespoons butter
    Salt and pepper to taste
    1 teaspoon nutmeg
    6 tablespoons light cream or milk
    Chopped parsley

Peel and slice or cube turnips and place in boiling salted water to cover. Boil uncovered for 15 to 30 minutes until tender. Peel potatoes and cook in boiling salted water until tender. Drain vegetables.

Place in a pot. Add butter and mash well. Add salt and pepper to taste. Stir in nutmeg. Add cream and beat well. Gently reheat if necessary.

Serve in a heated dish. Garnish with chopped parsley.

Leeks in Lemon Butter

INGREDIENTS:

12 leeks
2 cups chicken or beef bouillon
3 tablespoons butter
2 tablespoons lemon juice

Cut off green tops to tender portion of leeks and trim the roots. Wash thoroughly to remove sand.

Slice into 1-inch pieces.

Cook, covered, in bouillon until just tender (about 15 to 20 minutes). Drain thoroughly.

Place on a warm serving dish. Melt butter, add lemon juice. Pour over the leeks and serve.

Colcannon

INGREDIENTS:

1 medium cabbage
2 tablespoons butter
6 large potatoes, peeled and cut in half
1½ cups milk
2 scallions or leeks, finely chopped
Salt and white pepper to taste
Minced parsley

Peel potatoes and place in pan with enough cold water to cover. Add salt and boil until tender, 30-40 minutes. Drain well and shake potatoes in pan over heat for a few minutes to dry them. Mash the potatoes.

Meanwhile, core and shred cabbage. Boil in 2 cups of salted water until tender, approximately 8-10 minutes. Do not overcook. Drain well and toss with 2 tablespoons of melted butter. Cover loosely.

Chop scallions, finely, using bulb and the green tops. Pour milk into a small saucepan and add scallions. Bring to a boil. Pour the milk and scallions into the mashed potatoes. Add salt and pepper to taste. Beat until light and fluffy. Fold in the cabbage and heat over moderately low heat, adding more milk if necessary.

Mound the mixture in a heated serving dish. Make a well in the center, add butter to taste and let melt. Garnish with minced fresh parsley.

Curly Kale

INGREDIENTS:

1½ lbs. curly kale
3 cups boiling water
3 tablespoons butter
Salt and pepper
Nutmeg

Wash kale under running water. Discard tough stalks and remove any withered leaves. Wash again in cold water. Strip leaves from midrib.

Cook covered, in boiling salted water, approximately 10-12 minutes.

Drain well and toss in butter or margarine. Season to taste with salt and pepper and a pinch of nutmeg.

Emily's Cabbage Salad

INGREDIENTS:

1 medium cabbage, shredded (reserve green outer leaves)
2 apples, peeled and chopped
3 medium carrots, shredded
2 tablespoons chopped onion
2 stalks celery, chopped
½ cup raisins
5 tablespoons mayonnaise
3 tablespoons milk
Salt and pepper to taste
1 sliced unpeeled apple

Combine cabbage, apples, carrots, onions, celery and raisins in large mixing bowl. In small bowl, blend mayonnaise with milk, salt and pepper. Pour dressing over salad and toss. Arrange on cabbage lined serving platter and garnish with apple slices.

Maureen's Cauliflower

INGREDIENTS:

>1 medium cauliflower
>Juice of ½ lemon
>2-4 slices of cooked bacon, crumbled
>1 cup fresh bread crumbs
>2 tablespoons butter
>Salt and pepper

Remove leaves and peel stems thinly. Leave whole or break into flowerets.

Cook in a small amount of water with lemon juice. Cover tightly and cook until just tender. Drain well.

Fry bacon until crisp and crumble. Sauté bread crumbs in 2-3 tablespoons butter.

Mix bacon, crumbs, salt and pepper and sprinkle over cauliflower.

Cashel Beets

INGREDIENTS:

>1 bunch beets
>5 tablespoons butter
>1 small onion, finely sliced
>¼ cup vinegar
>1 teaspoon sugar
>½ teaspoon dry mustard
>Salt and pepper to taste
>Chopped parsley

Cut off tops of beets, leaving 2 inches. Wash well and leave whole. Place in boiling water, using enough water to cover. Cover and boil rapidly until tender, about 35 minutes.

Rub off skin under cold water. Cut off stems and slice beets.

Melt butter in saucepan, sauté onion gently until soft. Add vinegar, sugar, dry mustard and blend well. Season with salt and pepper to taste.

Add beets to liquid and reheat.

Serve garnished with chopped parsley.

BREADS

Rose McLoughlin's Barmbrack
(traditionally served on Halloween)

INGREDIENTS:

1 package dry yeast (¼ ounce)
1 ¼ cups milk
2 tablespoons sugar
4 cups flour
½ teaspoon cinnamon
¼ teaspoon nutmeg
2 tablespoons butter or margarine
2 eggs, well beaten
1 cup floured raisins

Preheat oven to 400°.

Dissolve yeast in ¼ cup of warmed milk and add 1 tablespoon of sugar. Set aside.

Sift dry ingredients together. Work butter into dry ingredients with a knife until it crumbles. Add 1 tablespoon of sugar, yeast liquid, well beaten eggs and 1 cup of warm milk.

Beat with wooden spoon until batter is stiff. Fold in floured raisins. Turn into buttered and floured 8-inch cake tin. Cover with cloth and let rise until double in bulk (about 1 hour). Keep in a warm place.

Bake at 400° for 1 hour.

Remove from pan and cool on a rack.

Bridget Billerman's Soda Bread

INGREDIENTS:

4 cups flour
1 ½ teaspoons salt
1 teaspoon baking soda
2 teaspoons baking powder
2 tablespoons sugar
1 tablespoon butter
1 ½ cups buttermilk or sour milk
1 cup raisins (optional)

Preheat oven to 375°

Mix dry ingredients together thoroughly. Cut in butter with knife.

Make a well in center and gradually mix in just enough buttermilk to make a soft but firm dough. Add raisins if desired. Shape into a ball. Knead on a floured surface for 2 to 3 minutes until dough is smooth. Form into a round loaf and with floured knife make a cross through center of the bread. Place on a buttered and floured baking sheet or cake tin.

Bake at 375° for 40 to 50 minutes.

TO SOUR MILK: Add one teaspoon of lemon juice to 2 cups of milk. Let stand for a few hours.

Mercedes' Guinness Bread
(an adaption of the popular beer bread)

INGREDIENTS:

2 packages of dry yeast
½ cup of warm water
1 tablespoon sugar
1 bottle of Guinness stout (6.3 oz.)
2 tablespoons honey
1 tablespoon margarine or butter
1 teaspoon caraway seeds
2 teaspoons salt
1 ½ cups whole wheat flour
2 ½ cups unsifted white flour
1 teaspoon ginger
1 tablespoon margarine or butter

Preheat oven to 375°.

Dissolve yeast in ½ cup of warm water and 1 tablespoon of sugar; set aside for five minutes. Heat stout, honey and margarine until warm. Add stout mix to the dissolved yeast and stir into 1 ½ cups of whole wheat flour. Beat until smooth. Stir in remaining flour, ginger and caraway seeds to make a soft dough.

Shape into a ball. Knead on a floured board until smooth, about 3 minutes. Form into a round loaf and with floured knife make a cross through center of the bread. Place in a greased 8-inch round cake tin. Cover with tea towel and let rise in a warm place for 1 hour. Bake at 375° for 30 minutes or until done. Remove from pan and brush with butter. Cool on rack.

Kinsale Bread

INGREDIENTS:

2 packages yeast (½ ounce)
2 cups warm water
2 tablespoons sugar
6 cups whole wheat flour
½ teaspoon salt
¼ cup molasses
½ cup honey

Preheat oven to 450°.

Dissolve yeast in ½ cup warm water and one tablespoon sugar. Set aside.

Take half of the flour and make a batter with the yeast mixture and 1 ½ cups of warm water. Cover the bowl with a damp cloth and let stand for 15 minutes.

Add the rest of the flour, salt, molasses, sugar and honey. Beat with a wooden spoon until batter is stiff. Knead on a floured surface for 10 minutes.

Lightly grease one large loaf pan. Place dough in pan. Cover and place in a warm spot for one hour or until dough doubles in volume.

Bake for 45 minutes, reversing position of the pan half-way through the cooking cycle.

Remove from oven and place on a wire rack. Let stand for 20 minutes. Remove from pan and cool thoroughly before cutting.

Grandmother Kate Cannon's Sweet Bread

INGREDIENTS:

3 cups flour
1 ½ teaspoons salt
¾ teaspoon baking soda
2 teaspoons baking powder
¼ cup sugar
4 tablespoons butter
1 cup raisins
1 egg
¼ cup molasses
1-1 ¼ cups buttermilk

Preheat oven to 325°.

Mix dry ingredients together. Cut in butter with knife or pastry blender. Add raisins. Beat the egg with fork and add to the molasses. Pour egg and molasses mixture into flour gradually. Add the buttermilk while stirring.

With floured hands form into a round cake. Bake in a lightly greased and floured cake tin at 325° for 1¼ hours.

Grandmother MacNeely's Whole-Grain Soda Bread

INGREDIENTS:

3 cups whole wheat flour
1 cup all purpose flour
1 ½ teaspoons salt
1 teaspoon baking soda
¾ teaspoon baking powder
1 ½-2 cups buttermilk

Preheat oven to 375°.

Mix all the dry ingredients thoroughly. Make a well in the center and gradually mix in just enough buttermilk to make a soft but firm dough. Shape the dough into a ball. Knead on a floured surface for 2 to 3 minutes until dough is smooth. Form into a round loaf and with floured knife make a cross through the center of the bread. Place in a well-buttered cake tin or on a cookie sheet.

Bake in preheated 375° oven for 35 to 40 minutes or until nicely browned. If bread sounds hollow when rapped on the bottom with knuckles, it is baked. Let cool before slicing.

Grandmother Mary MacNeely's three-legged pot is still in use. Traditionally, the bread was baked in such a pot over the turf fire. Katie Mangan, until recently, continued to do her daily baking in the same manner.

Meighan's Brown Tea Scones

INGREDIENTS:

1 ¾ cups flour
1 ¾ cups whole wheat flour
½ teaspoon salt
2 teaspoons baking powder
2 tablespoons sugar
4 tablespoons butter
1 egg, beaten
1 cup milk

Preheat oven to 425°.

Mix flour and whole wheat flour thoroughly. Add salt, baking powder and sugar and mix well. Rub in the butter with fingertips. Beat egg with fork and add to the milk. Mix in sufficient milk to make a soft dough. Shape into a ball with floured hands. Roll out to 1-inch thickness and cut into rounds with floured cutter. Place on a greased baking sheet and bake at 425° for approximately 20 minutes. When cool, break in half and spread with butter and/or strawberry jam.

Irene Gillespie's Scones

INGREDIENTS:

2 cups flour
¾ teaspoon baking soda
¾ teaspoon sugar
2 teaspoons baking powder
¾ teaspoon salt
4 tablespoons butter
¾ cup buttermilk

Preheat oven to 450°.

Sift together dry ingredients. Mix in butter with knife or pastry cutter. Pour in buttermilk. Stir into soft dough with wooden fork. Turn out and knead lightly on a floured board. Roll out to 1-inch thickness and cut into rounds with pastry cutter.

Place on ungreased baking sheet and bake at 450° for about 12 minutes until risen and lightly browned.

Serve warm with butter, marmalade or honey.

Delia's Oat Scones

INGREDIENTS:

½ cup butter or margarine, melted
⅓ cup milk
1 egg, beaten
¾ cup all purpose flour
1 cup whole wheat flour
1 cup Irish oatmeal
¼ cup sugar
1 tablespoon baking powder
1 teaspoon cream of tartar
½ teaspoon salt
½ cup golden raisins

Preheat oven to 425°.

Combine flours, oatmeal, sugar, baking powder, cream of tartar and salt in a mixing bowl. Add butter, milk and beaten egg to the dry ingredients. Mix until dry ingredients are moistened. Stir in raisins.

Shape dough to form a ball. Pat out on lightly floured surface to form 8-inch circle. Cut into 8 to 12 wedges or farls. Bake on greased baking sheet in preheated 425° oven for 12-15 minutes or until golden brown.

Serve warm with butter, preserves or honey.

Nancy's Honey Scones

INGREDIENTS:

4 cups all purpose flour
4 ½ teaspoons baking powder
1 teaspoon salt
½ cup butter or margarine
2 tablespoons sugar
½ cup currants
3 tablespoons honey
¾ cup milk

Preheat oven to 425°.

Sift flour, baking powder and salt into mixing bowl. Rub in butter. Mix in sugar and currants Add honey and milk and blend until a soft dough forms and flour is absorbed.

Place on floured board and knead quickly. Roll out to ½ inch thickness. Cut into rounds and place on greased baking sheet. Brush tops with milk or beaten egg.

Bake at 425° for 10–12 minutes until golden. Split and serve with butter or preserves.

Margaret's Quick Bread with Caraway Seeds

INGREDIENTS:

4 cups self-rising cake flour
1 teaspoon salt
2 tablespoons margarine
1 tablespoon caraway seeds
1 ¼ cups of milk

Preheat oven to 425°.

Grease and flour 8-inch loaf tin.

Sift flour and salt, rub in the margarine and add caraway seeds. Make a well in the center and add milk all at once. Mix with fork to form soft dough.

Turn out on floured board and knead until smooth. Place in 8-inch loaf tin. Cut a cross on top, using a sharp knife. Brush with milk.

Bake at 425° for 40–50 minutes until light golden brown.

Honor's Oatmeal Bread

INGREDIENTS:

½ cup warm milk
¼ cup boiling water
¼ cup butter or margarine
¼ cup honey
1 teaspoon salt
1 package of dry yeast (¼ ounce)
½ cup warm water
1 tablespoon sugar
1 cup Irish oatmeal
3 cups whole wheat flour
1 egg, beaten

Preheat oven to 375°.

Combine warm milk, boiling water, butter, honey and salt in large bowl. Stir until butter melts.

Dissolve yeast in ½ cup warm water with 1 tablespoon sugar. Let stand for 5 minutes.

Add dissolved yeast, oatmeal, flour and egg to water and milk mixture. Stir until batter is stiff (more flour may be added if batter is not stiff enough). Knead for a few minutes. Cover with foil. Let rise in a warm place for 1 hour or until double in bulk.

Place risen dough in a greased and floured 8-inch cake tin. Let rise again in a warm place for 40 minutes.

Bake in preheated oven at 375° for 35-40 minutes or until golden brown.

Mary McLoughlin's Bannock

INGREDIENTS:

3 cups flour
1 teaspoon baking soda
1 teaspoon cream of tartar
1 tablespoon sugar
¾ cup raisins
1 ¼ cups buttermilk

Preheat oven to 400°.
Grease and flour 8-inch cake tin.
Place all dry ingredients in a bowl and blend until well mixed.
Pour buttermilk into center of flour and stir into a soft slightly sticky dough, using a wooden spoon.
Scrape dough into cake tin and spread roughly. Bake at 400° for 25-30 minutes until risen and lightly browned.

AFTERS

Ann MacNeely's Porter Cake

INGREDIENTS:

1 bottle of Guinness stout, 6.3 oz.
1 teaspoon baking soda
2 cups sugar
1 cup butter, softened
3 eggs, beaten
1 cups raisins
½ cup mixed candied peel
½ cup candied cherries, chopped
4 cups all purpose flour
1 teaspoon ginger

Preheat oven to 375°.
Butter and lightly flour 9 x 5-inch loaf pan.
Add 1 teaspoon of baking soda to 1 bottle of stout (stout should be at room temperature). Let stand for 5 minutes.
Cream the butter, slowly add the sugar and beat until light. Beat the eggs and add. Fold in the fruit and beat one minute. Stir in the flour and ginger and beat well. Add Guinness and baking soda mixture and continue to beat for five minutes. Turn into loaf pan and bake at 375° for 2 hours. Allow cake to ripen for 1 week before cutting/slicing.

Anita McCudden's Sweet Apple Flan

INGREDIENTS:

For the filling:
2 tablespoons butter
6 tablespoons sugar
Grated rind and juice of one lemon
5 cooking apples
1 egg, beaten
For the pastry:
1 ½ cups flour
1 teaspoon salt
½ cup margarine
¼ cup sugar
1 egg yolk, beaten
4 tablespoons cold water

PASTRY: Preheat oven to 400°. Sift the flour and salt. Rub in the butter until mixture resembles meal. Add sugar and mix well. Beat the egg yolk and add 4 tablespoons of cold water. Add to dough. Mix with a fork until the dough is stiff. Form into a ball and refrigerate for 1 hour.

FILLING: Melt the butter and stir in the sugar, grated rind and juice of lemon. Peel, core and chop the apples and stir into the butter and sugar. Mix in beaten egg and stir well. Turn the filling into a flan ring or pie plate.

ASSEMBLY: Roll out pastry dough and cover filling, brush with a little beaten egg or milk. Bake at 400° for 35 minutes.

Fionna's Quick Sponge Cake

INGREDIENTS:

> 2 cup self-raising flour
> 1 cup sugar
> 2 teaspoons baking powder
> 5 large eggs
> 1 cup margarine (8 oz.)
> For the filling:
>> 1¼ cup confectioner's sugar
>> 3 tablespoons butter, softened
>> 1 heaping teaspoon instant coffee
>> 2 tablespoons cream or Irish whiskey

Preheat oven to 350°.

Grease and flour 2 9-inch cake tins. Put all ingredients into bowl. With an electric mixer, beat at medium speed until well blended. Beat at high speed for 3 minutes.

Bake at 350° for 30 minutes.

Cool on rack.

FILLING: Blend sugar, butter, coffee and liquid together until smooth and creamy.

ASSEMBLY: Place bottom layer of sponge on serving plate and spread filling evenly. Top with second layer and dust with confectioner's sugar.

Turlough Cheese Cake

INGREDIENTS:

Pastry:

    1 cup plus 1 tablespoon flour
    ½ teaspoon salt
    1 tablespoon sugar
    3 tablespoons butter
    3 tablespoons iced water

Filling:

    1 lb. uncreamed cottage cheese
    2 eggs
    3 tablespoons sugar
    Grated peel and juice of 1 large lemon

Topping:

    1 egg
    1 tablespoon flour
    1 tablespoon sugar
    1 tablespoon melted butter
    1 can mandarin oranges, drained

PASTRY: Mix flour, salt and sugar. Cut butter into flour with pastry blender until it resembles meal. Sprinkle pastry with water and blend lightly with a fork. Shape into a ball and refrigerate at least 1 hour.

FILLING: Separate two eggs. Beat yolks lightly with fork and add to cottage cheese. Add sugar, lemon rind and juice and beat. Beat egg whites until stiff and fold into cottage cheese mixture.

Roll out pastry to fit a 9-inch pie dish. Put filling into pastry shell. For the topping, beat egg lightly with fork and add sugar, flour and melted butter. Stir well and pour evenly over the top of cake.

Bake at 350° for 1 hour. Turn off heat and leave in oven for a further 30 minutes with oven door open.

When cool, decorate with drained mandarin orange sections.

Emily Gillespie's Rhubarb Meringue Tart

INGREDIENTS:

For the pastry:
- 2 cups flour
- 1 teaspoon salt
- ⅔ cup margarine or butter
- 5 tablespoons of cold water

For the filling:
- 3 cups diced rhubard
- 1 cup sugar
- ¼ teaspoon salt
- 2 tablespoons water
- 1 ½ tablespoons cornstarch
- 4 eggs

For the meringue:
- 2 egg whites
- 4 tablespoons sugar

FOR THE PASTRY: Place 2 cups of flour, 1 teaspoon of salt in a bowl and blend. Rub in ⅔ cup butter or margarine until mixture looks like fine bread crumbs. Then add 4 tablespoons of ice cold water and mix with fork until the dough is stiff. Form into a ball and refrigerate for 30 minutes. Roll out pastry dough and place in 9 inch pie plate or flan ring. Prick the pastry with a fork all over. Bake at 450° for about 15 minutes or until lightly browned. Remove from oven and cool before adding filling.

FOR THE FILLING: Combine 3 cups rhubarb, 1 cup sugar, salt and 2 tablespoons of water in a saucepan. Place over low heat and cook for about five minutes or until tender. Dissolve cornstarch in 3 tablespoons of cold water and stir into the rhubarb mixture. Cook, stirring constantly, until clear and thickened.

Beat the egg yolks slightly; stir a little of hot rhubarb into them. Stir eggs into the remainder of the rhubarb. Cool. Beat two egg whites until stiff but not dry. Fold into rhubarb mixture. Pour into cooled baked shell. Top with meringue.

FOR THE MERINQUE: Whip egg whites until stiff. Add the sugar and whip until stiff. Pile the meringue over the rhubarb and bake at 325° for 20 minutes or until meringue is golden.

Grace Glynn's Half-Penny Pudding
INGREDIENTS:

 2 cups fine bread crumbs (freshly made)
 1 teaspoon allspice
 1 cup sugar
 1 cup flour
 1 apple, cored, sliced and peeled
 1 cup raisins
 1 cup sultanas (golden raisins)
 1 cup chopped candied peel
 ¾ cup butter
 4 eggs
 For the sauce:
   1 cup powdered sugar
   4 tablespoons butter
   1 egg
   1 teaspoon lemon juice or spirits

Cream the butter with the allspice and sugar. Add crumbs, flour, eggs and mix. Add fruits and mix well to separate.

Fill a greased 1 ½ quart mold about two-thirds full and cover with lid or foil. If foil, tie tightly with string. Stand on a rack in an inch of boiling water in a pot with a tight cover. Steam 1 ½ hours, adding more boiling water if necessary. Serve warm or cold with sauce.

SAUCE: Beat until soft 5 tablespoons butter. Add 1 cup sugar gradually and beat until well blended. Add lemon juice. Beat in one egg and continue beating until smooth. Chill.

Irish Coffee Mousse
INGREDIENTS:

 1 ½ tablespoons instant coffee dissolved in 1 cup of water or 1
    cup very strong coffee
 6 eggs, separated
 ¾ cup sugar
 ¼ cup Irish whiskey
 2 packages unflavored gelatin
 1 ¼ cups heavy cream
 2 tablespoons slivered almonds

In one quart saucepan, blend coffee in water and add 6 beaten egg yolks, then ¾ cup sugar and ¼ cup Irish whiskey. Sprinkle gelatin evenly over mixture. Cook over low heat, stirring constantly, until gelatin is completely dissolved. Cover and refrigerate until mixture mounds when dropped from a spoon, about 45 minutes.

In small bowl, with mixer at high speed, beat egg whites until soft peaks form.

In large bowl, with mixer at medium speed, beat 1 cup heavy cream until stiff peaks form.

Fold egg whites into whipped cream and blend well. Fold into coffee mixture.

Spoon the mousse into a crystal bowl and chill until ready to serve. Beat remaining ¼ cup of cream. When ready to serve, garnish with whipped cream and slivered almonds.

Irish Mist Pudding

INGREDIENTS:

3 ounces unsweetened chocolate
¼ cup Irish Mist
1 tablespoon instant coffee
¾ cup sugar
⅛ teaspoon salt
3 egg yolks
1 ¼ cups heavy cream, reserve ¼ cup for garnish

Combine chocolate, Irish Mist and coffee in small saucepan. Cook gently over low heat until the chocolate melts. Add sugar and salt, stirring until sugar dissolves. Remove from heat and cool.

Beat egg yolks, add cooled chocolate mixture and stir over low heat until smooth.

Whip cream until stiff. Reserve ¼ cup for garnish. Fold the remaining cream into the chocolate mixture. Spoon into six Irish coffee glasses and chill. Garnish with remaining whipped cream and serve.

Angela Padden's St. Patrick's Day Trifle

INGREDIENTS:

10-12 ladyfingers or sponge cake in equivalent amount
¼ cup seedless raspberry or apricot jam
¼ cup sherry (optional)
1 package of lime gelatin (6 oz.)
1 can of pears, drained, syrup reserved
½ pint whipping cream
2 oz. of slivered almonds

Line the bottom of a glass dessert bowl with some of the ladyfingers which have been split in half and spread with jam. Pour the sherry over these and let stand for ½ hour. Dissolve gelatin in 2 cups of boiling water, stirring until clear. Stir in 1½ cups of reserved syrup and allow to set slightly. Slice the pears and arrange some of them on top of the ladyfingers. Put on second layer of ladyfingers and fruit. Continue like this, using all the ladyfingers and fruit. Pour gelatin over all and refrigerate until set. Beat the cream until thick, pile on top of the trifle and decorate with slivered almonds.

Emily's Holiday Trifle

INGREDIENTS:

12 ladyfingers, split
¼ cup seedless raspberry or strawberry jam
2 ⅛ cups fresh or frozen raspberries, strawberries or sliced
    peaches (reserve ⅛ cup for decoration)
For the custard:
    2 cups milk
    4 egg yolks
    ½ cup sugar
    3 tablespoons cornstarch
    1 ½ teaspoons vanilla
    ½ pint whipping cream
    ¼ cup slivered almonds

Split ladyfingers and spread with jam. Arrange a layer of ladyfingers in glass dessert bowl and top with ⅓ of the fruit (reserve ⅛ cup of fruit for decoration).

TO PREPARE CUSTARD: Warm the milk, but do not let it boil. Beat the egg yolks in large bowl and slowly add the sugar. Mix in 3 tablespoons of cornstarch. Gradually add the warm milk, while stirring. Return to the pan and stir over low heat until the custard thickens. Do not allow to boil. Remove the custard from heat, cook slightly and add vanilla. Cool the finished custard for 30 minutes.

Spoon ⅓ of the custard over the ladyfingers. Arrange another layer of ladyfingers, fruit and custard. Top with another layer of ladyfingers, fruit and custard.

Whip cream until stiff and spread over the trifle. Arrange reserved fruit and almonds in a design on the cream.

Bea Naughton's Spice Cake

INGREDIENTS:

- 2 cups brown sugar
- 2 cups hot water
- 2 tablespoons butter or margarine
- 1 15-oz. package raisins
- 1 teaspoon salt
- ½ teaspoon cloves
- 1 teaspoon cinnamon
- ½ teaspoon nutmeg
- 3 cups flour
- 1 teaspoon baking soda
- 1 teaspoon baking powder

Preheat oven to 350°.

Place sugar, water, butter, raisins, salt and spices together in a heavy saucepan and blend. Bring to a boil, then simmer for 5 minutes. Allow to cool.

Sift flour, baking soda and baking powder together. Stir into cooled mixture. Mix until all ingredients are well blended.

Bake in a lined loaf tin for 1 ½ hours at 350°.

TO LINE LOAF TIN: Cut double thickness of wax paper to fit bottom and sides of loaf tin.

Rhubarb Compote

INGREDIENTS:

2 ½ cups rhubarb, cut into 2 inch pieces
⅓ cup sugar
¾ cup water
¼ teaspoon ginger
For custard sauce:
    4 eggs
    ½ cup sugar
    2 cups milk
    1 teaspoon vanilla

Trim ends of rhubarb, discard the leaves and wash well. Cut into 2 inch pieces without peeling.

Dissolve sugar in ¾ cup of water, bring to a boil and continue boiling for 3 minutes. Add rhubarb and ginger. Reduce heat and simmer gently until tender. Chill.

TO MAKE CUSTARD: Beat eggs in a bowl. Heat the milk in a saucepan and add sugar. Pour heated milk on the beaten eggs, stirring to prevent curdling. Return to pan and stir continuously over low heat until custard thickens. Add vanilla and blend. Chill.

TO ASSEMBLE: Place rhubarb in individual sherbet glasses or fruit bowls. Spoon custard sauce on top of rhubarb.

Kathleen's Honey Nut Ring

INGREDIENTS:

¾ cup margarine or butter, softened
⅓ cup sugar
3 tablespoons honey
3 large eggs, separated
2 cups all purpose flour
1 teaspoon cinnamon
½ teaspoon nutmeg
½ cup chopped walnuts
4 tablespoons orange juice
Grated rind of one orange

Preheat oven to 375°.

Grease and flour an 8 ½" x 2" cake ring.

Cream margarine and sugar together until light and fluffy. Using a wooden spoon, beat in the honey. Beat the egg yolks into the mixture, mixing thoroughly. Sift dry ingredients and fold into the batter. Add walnuts, orange juice and grated rind. Beat egg whites until stiff and fold into the batter.

Pour into prepared tin and bake at 375° for 45 minutes. Cool on rack.

Golden Vale Cottage Cheese

INGREDIENTS:

1 ½ lbs. cottage cheese
6 tablespoons butter, softened
½ cup sugar
3 eggs
¼ teaspoon cinnamon
½ pint heavy cream
⅛ teaspoon vanilla
1 pint strawberries, blueberries or sliced fruit in season
2 tablespoons Irish Mist (optional)
2 tablespoons slivered almonds

Blend cottage cheese, butter, sugar and cinnamon together. Separate eggs. Beat yolks with fork and stir into cottage cheese. Beat egg whites until stiff and add to cottage cheese mixture. Whip the cream until stiff and fold in vanilla. Blend into cottage cheese mixture.

Pour half of the mixture into a glass bowl, cover with the fruit. Add remaining cottage cheese mixture. Spoon the Irish Mist over the pudding and garnish with slivered almonds. Chill.

Serve in sherbet glasses.

Connemarra Apple Cake

INGREDIENTS:

2½ cups flour
1 teaspoon baking soda
⅛ teaspoon salt
¾ cup sugar
6 tablespoons butter
¾ cups sour milk *
1 egg, beaten
2 apples, peeled and chopped

Preheat oven to 375°.
Grease and flour 8-inch cake tin.

Sift the flour, baking powder, salt and sugar into a mixing bowl. Rub the butter into the flour mixture. Add the beaten egg and sour milk gradually and blend. Fold in the peeled and chopped apples.

Spread the mixture into the prepared cake tin and bake for 45 minutes at 375°.

* For directions on how to sour milk, see page 71 [Bridget Billerman's soda bread].

Theresa's Coffee Cake

INGREDIENTS:

¾ cup margarine or butter, softened
¾ cup sugar
3 large eggs
1½ cups self-rising cake flour, sifted
1 teaspoon instant coffee dissolved in 1 tablespoon
    hot water
For the frosting:
    6 tablespoons margarine, softened
    2 cups confectioners' sugar, sifted
    1 teaspoon instant coffee dissolved in 1 tablespoon hot water
    1 tablespoon milk
    ¼ cup chopped walnuts

Preheat oven to 350°.

Grease and flour 2 8-inch cake tins.

Sift flour, add margarine, sugar, eggs and coffee. Beat until smooth (about 1 to 2 minutes with electric beater at medium speed, or 3 to 4 minutes by hand).

Pour into prepared tins and bake at 350° for 25–35 minutes. Cool in the pan on a rack for about 5 minutes. Remove from pan and cool thoroughly before frosting.

FOR THE FROSTING: Cream margarine, add sifted sugar gradually, stirring until well blended. Stir in the coffee and milk; beat until smooth.

After frosting cake, decorate with chopped walnuts.

Jacqueline's Baked Apple Crumble

INGREDIENTS:

8 cooking apples
1 tablespoon butter
¼ cup sugar
2-3 tablespoons water
For the topping:
½ cup butter, softened
½ cup sugar
¾ cup all purpose flour
¾ cup oatmeal, quick oats or Irish oatmeal
¼ teaspoon cinnamon
¼ teaspoon cloves

Preheat oven to 350°.

Butter 9-inch pie dish.

Peel, core and thinly slice the apples. Layer the sliced apples in the prepared pie dish. Sprinkle with ¼ cup of sugar. Add 2-3 tablespoons water.

FOR THE TOPPING: Cream butter and ½ cup sugar, add flour, oatmeal and spices. Blend until the mixture resembles fine breadcrumbs.

Pile the crumb mixture on top of the apples.

Bake for 30-40 minutes at 350°.

Anita's Chocolate Potato Cake

INGREDIENTS:

2½ cups sifted self-rising cake flour
1 teaspoon cinnamon
¼ teaspoon ground cloves
¼ teaspoon nutmeg
⅔ cup margarine or butter, softened
2 cups sugar
3 eggs
½ cup chopped almonds
3 ozs. unsweetened chocolate, melted
1 cup mashed potatoes
⅔ cup milk
For the Frosting:
    2 cups sifted confectioners' sugar
    2 tablespoons butter, softened
    Juice and rind of one orange

Preheat oven to 350°.

Sift flour and spices. Cream butter and sugar, beating until light and fluffy. Add eggs and beat well. Blend in nuts and melted chocolate. Add mashed potatoes and beat thoroughly. Add flour mix alternately with milk, a small amount at a time, beating after each addition. Beat until smooth.

Bake in two greased and floured 8-inch cake tins at 350° for 50 minutes.

Cool cake in pans for 10 minutes. Turn onto wire racks and cool completely before frosting.

FOR THE FROSTING: Blend confectioners' sugar and butter. Beat in orange juice and rind. Beat until smooth.

Laura's Baked Carrot Pudding

INGREDIENTS:

1 cup finely shredded carrots
1 cup flour
½ cup brown sugar
1 teaspoon baking soda
1 teaspoon baking powder
1 teaspoon ginger
1 teaspoon nutmeg
1 teaspoon cinnamon
3 tablespoons butter or margarine
1 egg
1 cup buttermilk
1 cup raisins
½ cup chopped nuts
1 cup heavy cream, whipped
3 tablespoons grated orange rind

Preheat oven to 350°.
Grease a 1½ quart casserole.
Grate carrots finely or shred in food processor.
Place all dry ingredients into a mixing bowl and blend thoroughly.
Melt butter in skillet, add carrots and sauté over medium heat until carrots are tender (cover the pan with lid to retain moisture).
Beat egg lightly with a fork, add to the buttermilk and blend. Combine with dry ingredients and mix thoroughly with a wooden spoon. Fold in carrots, raisins and nuts.
Turn into greased baking dish and bake at 350° for 40 to 45 minutes until firm.
Fold grated orange rind into whipped cream.
Serve pudding warm, topped with the whipped cream.

Charles McSpiritt's Christmas Pudding

INGREDIENTS:

1 cup dark raisins
1 cup golden raisins
1 cup currants
1 cup chopped candied fruit
1 cup all purpose flour
½ teaspoon mace
1 teaspoon ginger
½ teaspoon cinnamon
Pinch of salt
1 cup brown sugar
2 oz. brandy or cider
1 cup bread crumbs
2 cups finely chopped suet
¼ cup ground almonds
Juice and rind of 1 lemon
1 tablespoon molasses
3 eggs
Milk to moisten
For the hard sauce:
    1 cup confectioners' sugar
    3 tablespoons butter, softened
    1 egg
    1 tablespoon whiskey or orange juice

Blanch raisins and currants by covering with boiling water. Let stand for ten minutes. Drain and place in a large bowl. Sift flour with spices and salt. Combine with raisins, currants and candied fruit. Add sugar, brandy, bread crumbs, suet, almonds, lemon juice and rind, molasses and mix well.

Beat eggs and stir into batter. Mix thoroughly so that all ingredients are well blended. If necessary, moisten with a little milk to make a dropping consistency.

Pour mixture into two 1 quart molds or heatproof bowls (containers should be only ⅔ full). Cover with double thickness of waxed paper and tie tightly.

Place mold on trivet in large pot filled with one inch of boiling water. Cover pot and simmer for 6 hours, adding more water if necessary.

Cool and wrap well for storing.

Steam for 1-2 hours before serving.

When serving, pour a little whiskey over pudding and light. Serve hard sauce in a small serving bowl.

FOR THE HARD SAUCE: Sift sugar and add butter. Beat until well blended. Beat in egg and add 1 tablespoon whiskey or juice. Beat until smooth.

Avoca Blackberry Cake

INGREDIENTS:

½ cup butter, softened
½ cup sugar
1 egg
2 cups all purpose flour
2 teaspoons baking powder
¼ teaspoon salt
½ cup milk
2 cups blackberries or 1 17-oz. can, drained
For the topping:
¼ cup butter, softened
½ cup sugar
¾ cup all purpose flour
½ teaspoon cinnamon

Preheat oven to 350°.

Grease and flour a 7-inch square cake pan.

Cream butter and sugar and beat in egg. Sift flour with baking powder and salt. Gradually add flour to butter and sugar. Add milk and beat to smooth batter.

Pour into prepared tin. Place washed and dried blackberries on top of the batter. (If using canned blackberries, drain well).

FOR THE TOPPING: Cream the butter and sugar. Add flour and cinnamon, blend until mixture crumbles. Sprinkle over blackberries. Bake at 350° for 1 hour.

Cool cake in pan on wire rack for 5 to 10 minutes before removing from pan.

Traditional Almond Tarts

INGREDIENTS:

1½ cups flour
1 egg separated
½ cup ground almonds (2 oz)
⅓ cup sugar
¼ teaspoon almond extract
¼ teaspoon baking soda
¼ teaspoon cream of tartar
1 teaspoon semolina
Raspberry jam
For the crust:
   1 tablespoon sugar
   4 tablespoons butter or margarine
   2-3 tablespoons water
   1 egg yolk, reserve egg white

Preheat oven to 350°.

FOR THE CRUST: Place flour and sugar in mixing bowl and blend. Cut in butter. Combine egg yolk with cold water and blend with fork. Add yolk to flour and stir with fork until mixture forms a ball. Chill for ½ hour.

When chilled, roll out pastry thinly on a floured surface. Cut into circles to line 12 tart or muffin tins.

FOR THE FILLING: Separate egg, reserve white. Place yolk in a bowl and beat with fork. Add almonds, sugar, almond extract, baking soda, cream of tartar and semolina. Mix until well blended. Beat both reserved egg whites until stiff and fold into almond mixture.

Line tins with pastry dough. Place ½ teaspoon raspberry jam in center of each pastry. Divide filling so that each tart is ¾ full.

Bake at 350° for 20 minutes or until set and pale golden.